God's Alphabet
for Life

God's Alphabet for Life

Devotions for Young Children

by
Joel R. Beeke
Heidi Boorsma

REFORMATION HERITAGE BOOKS
Grand Rapids, Michigan

God's Alphabet for Life
©2000, 2009 by Joel R. Beeke and Heidi Boorsma

Published by
Reformation Heritage Books
2965 Leonard St. NE
Grand Rapids, MI 49525
616-977-0889 / Fax 616-285-3246
e-mail: orders@heritagebooks.org
website: www.heritagebooks.org

Printed in the United States of America
13 14 15 16 17 18/10 9 8 7 6 5 4 3 2

Library of Congress Cataloging-in-Publication Data

Beeke, Joel R., 1952-
 God's alphabet for life : devotions for young children / by Joel R.
Beeke, Heidi Boorsma.
     p. cm.
 ISBN 978-1-60178-068-3 (pbk. : alk. paper)
 1. Christian children—Prayers and devotions. 2. English
language—Alphabet—Juvenile literature. 3. Christian life—Biblical
teaching—Juvenile literature. I. Boorsma, Heidi. II. Title.
 BV4870.B4278 2009
 242'.62—dc22
                                          2009035614

---

*For additional Reformed literature, request a free book list from
Reformation Heritage Books at the above address.*

Contents

Introduction

Young children,

    Do you know that you own something that is priceless? This treasure that you own is worth more than all of the clothes, food, and toys that you have. It is more valuable than the home where you live. In fact, it is worth more than the whole world! The priceless thing that you own is your soul—the spiritual part of you that you cannot see. You can see your body and touch your skin. But there is a part of you that you cannot see. This part of you is called your soul. When your body dies, your soul continues to live forever. Because your soul lives forever, it is very important.

Because our souls are so important, God says, "Keep thy soul diligently" (Deuteronomy 4:9). God then tells us that the way to be diligent in taking care of our souls is to remember the things that God has taught us. And this is why Psalm 119:11 says, "Thy word have I hid in mine heart, that I might not sin against thee." It is very important for us to know that the main way to take care of our souls is to believe and treasure what God has to say to us in the Bible.

The book that you are reading gives a number of Bible verses for you to hide in your heart. Because the Bible is important for the life of your soul, and because each Bible verse in this devotional book begins with a different letter of the

alphabet, we call this book *God's Alphabet for Life*. As you read this book, we want to encourage you to do a few things to help hide these Bible verses in your heart.

First, try to memorize the Bible verses at the beginning of each devotional. It is hard to hide something we do not have. In the same way, it is hard to hide verses in your heart if there are not verses there. So, pray for God to help you remember the Bible verses. Keep saying them until you can remember the words without looking.

Second, try to understand the Bible verses. If we memorize something but do not know what it means, then we have only stored letters and sounds in our head. So, try to think about each verse that you memorize. We explain each of the verses for you in this devotional. Pray that God would help you understand His Word.

Third, trust the verses that you memorize. We hide things that are important to us because we do not want them to slip away. In order to hide God's Word in your heart, it must be very important to you. Your soul will not get much good from the Bible if you do not trust God to use it to save you from your sin. Pray to God and ask Him to help you believe His Word with all your heart. Also, ask Him to use His Word to bring life to your soul.

If you believe that your soul is the most valuable thing you own, you will be sure to take care of it. This little book can help you guard your heart. We pray that God will use it to save your heart from the evil works of sin. Will you also pray that God will help you guard your heart as you hide His Word there?

Ask, and it
shall be
given you.

— MATTHEW 7:7a

DEAR CHILDREN, have you ever wondered how many books there are in the world? There are so many it seems as though it would be impossible to count them. There is one book that is different from all the other books in the world. This book is very special—it is the Bible.

What makes the Bible so special and different from all the other books? The Bible is special because it is God's Word. Other books are the thoughts and words of people, but the Bible is, from the beginning to the end, the thoughts and words of a holy God. God did not write the Bible Himself with His own hand, but He put His words within the minds and hearts of many different men, and He told them to write these words down.

The Bible is a perfect book. There are no mistakes in it, because God is a perfect God.

God gave us the Bible so that we may learn from it who we are and who God is. God tells us many things about who He is in the Bible. Most importantly, God's Word teaches us that we are lost sinners who have believed Satan's lies, and that there is only one way to become a child of God, through God's Son, Jesus Christ.

The Bible is like a treasure chest that God has given us. If someone were to give you a chest filled with treasures, you would open it right away. You would look at and hold everything in the chest. Children, did you know that when we hold the Bible in our hands, we are holding a great treasure? When we open God's Word and read it, we find that it is filled with precious promises. Promises mean a lot to us, don't they? If your mother promises to give you something special that you must wait for, do you not often ask her, "Mother, may I have it now? You promised that you would give it to me. How long must I wait?" You are so eager for her to give it to you that you continually remind her of her promise. It would be wrong for her to break her promise, wouldn't it? Sometimes parents and children do break their promises, but God *never* breaks His promises. It is impossible for God to do that. It would be sinful, and God cannot sin, for He is a perfect and holy God.

"Ask, and it shall be given you" (Matthew 7:7a) is one of God's great promises. Does this mean that whatever we ask for, God will give? No, but it does mean that if we truly need something for our soul or body, God not only *invites* us but *commands* us to pray to Him for it. If God thinks that it is necessary that we have something, then He will supply our need.

Do we have to ask only one time? No, God desires that we keep asking until we receive the things He knows we need. Pray often for the one thing everyone must receive, a new heart that hates sin, listens to God, believes in Jesus Christ alone for salvation, and loves Him.

Be ye kind one to another.

— EPHESIANS 4:32a

DEAR CHILDREN, did you know that even if someone is mean to us we must be kind to them? Many times our being kind to them makes them feel bad for being so mean to us!

Let's pretend you are playing with a toy at school. A boy named Nick takes the toy away from you. In your heart, you want to go to Nick, grab the toy, perhaps even push him, but this is not what God commands us to do. God commands us to be kind, so instead, you should first ask the Lord to help you obey His Word to be kind. Then you should say, "Nick, I had that toy first. If you would have asked me, I would have shared it with you. If you will be nice to me, I would like to play with you and share all of these toys with you." Saying this to Nick might make him feel amazed that you are being kind to him after he had been mean to you. He probably will feel sorry for having taken your toy.

In some ways, this is what happens when God's children sin against Him. God shows them how kind He has been to them. He has given them a new heart and all that they need for their body and soul. He has never treated them unkindly. When they think about this, they feel very unhappy for sinning against such a kind God. Ask God to make you truly sorry for treating your Creator so sinfully by all of the naughty things you do while He takes such good care of you and keeps calling you to repent and believe in His Son.

Create in me
a clean heart,
O God.

— PSALM 51:10a

WE ARE ALL BORN with a physical heart in our body, and we can feel it beating. It keeps us alive.

We are also born with a soul, but we cannot see it. The Bible sometimes calls our soul a heart, because just as our physical heart is the center of our physical life, so our soul is the center of our spiritual life. When David prays, "Create in me a clean heart, O God," he is asking God to make his soul, or spiritual heart, clean.

Our soul, or spiritual heart, is the center of who we really are. Our soul will go on living even after our bodies are buried in the ground. Where will we go on living? Well, if we have a clean soul, or spiritual heart, then we will live in heaven forever; but if our spiritual heart has never been made clean by Jesus' blood, we will go to hell forever.

Heaven is the kingdom where God lives. The Bible tells us it is a beautiful kingdom without sorrow or pain or tears. Hell is a terrible kingdom where Satan lives, and where sorrow, pain, and tears never stop.

But children, the sad thing is that we often think that we are good people. We believe that our spiritual heart is clean enough and we don't need any help. We do not pray to God, "Create in me a clean heart, O God."

If we are feeling fine, we do not need to go to the doctor; but if we become very sick and want to be better, we will gladly go to the doctor with the hope that, with God's bless-ing, he may be able to help us. Our spiritual heart is no differ-ent. If God shows us how dirty our hearts are with sin, then we will call to Him, because we will hate sin the way God hates it. We will be sorry that we have of-fended such a good God, so we will pray, "Create in me a clean heart, O God."

God is able and willing to give clean spiritual

hearts to boys and girls because of who Jesus is and what He has done. He does that when He teaches us to be very sorry for our sins, which we call repentance. He gives us to trust only in Jesus Christ for salvation and for a clean heart, which we call faith. Ask the Holy Spirit to bless God's Word to your spiritual heart, so that you may repent and believe in Jesus Christ alone for salvation. Then your spiritual heart will be made clean in Christ.

Depart from evil, and do good.

— PSALM 37:27a

GOD GIVES US good commands for good reasons. God wants sinners like us to honor Him and to live in heaven with Him. In this verse God is telling us not to do evil things. Now, evil things are what Satan—God's greatest enemy—likes and God hates, things that are disobedient to God's good law.

Satan likes to try to keep us so busy that we forget about God and forget to pray to Him. Satan doesn't have to work very hard at this, does he? He knows that he can keep us very busy with sports, games, new toys, and other things so that we go the whole day without thinking about God who made us and who is listening to hear if we are praying to Him. Satan is very happy if we crawl into bed at night and we have not prayed at all during the day. He is afraid we might ask God for a new heart and for faith to trust only in Jesus Christ for salvation. Satan does not want us to have those things. Satan knows that if we have a new heart, so that we truly repent of our sins and trust in Jesus Christ alone for salvation, we will go to heaven when we die. He will lose us as his prisoners.

Take time during the day to pray to God, asking Him to help you do what is good. God never sleeps. He likes to hear children praying to Him.

Even a child is known by his doings.

— PROVERBS 20:11a

THIS BIBLE VERSE was written by the wisest man who ever lived. The man's name was Solomon, and he was the new king of a country called Judah. One night the Lord came to Solomon in a dream and spoke to him. God said to Solomon, "Ask what I shall give thee" (1 Kings 3:5b).

If we were asked that question, perhaps some of us would answer "money," because then we could buy whatever we wanted. But Solomon did not ask for money. He asked for wisdom. Since Solomon was a king ruling many people, he felt he needed wisdom to answer their questions and to make many decisions. God was pleased with

Solomon's request, so He not only gave him wisdom but also riches and honor. People came from faraway countries to hear the wise things that Solomon had to say. Because Solomon loved God, he used the riches and wisdom that God gave him to build a new temple where the people could worship God.

Children, remember that God not only knows what grown-ups are doing, but His all-searching eye is watching you every moment. He sees all that you do and hears all that you say. Ask God to give you wisdom, like Solomon, to keep you from sin and to help you seek God.

Fear God, and keep his commandments.

— ECCLESIASTES 12:13b

F

MOST OF THE TIME when we hear the word "fear" we think of being very afraid of something. But that is not what fear means here. To fear God means to love and respect God.

Love and respect for God is like love and respect for our parents. If there is a father who is very kind and gentle to his child, do you think that child would try to hurt his father's feelings by doing naughty things all the time, making his father sad and upset? No, if that child truly loves his kind and gentle father, he will try to please him and do what is right and good. If the child does something wrong, he will feel so bad for hurting his dear father that he will come with a heavy heart and tears to tell him he is sorry for what he did. This is to "fear" our parents. God commands us to fear our parents in His holy law. He says in the fifth commandment, "Honor thy father and thy mother."

God is so good to His children that He gives them everything they need: food, clothing, and a home to live in. If they come into trouble or hard times, they ask God for help. He says in His word, "And call upon me in the day of trouble: I will deliver thee, and thou shalt glorify me" (Psalm 50:15). Above all, He gives them His Word, the Bible, and His Son, the Lord Jesus Christ. Because of Christ, who is their Savior, they learn to love and respect God as a heavenly Father. This should make us eager to be God's children, so that we ask Him, "Oh Lord, make me one of Thy blessed children."

Ask the Lord to give you this fear of God in your heart so that you will be sad and repent when you sin against His commandments. There are ten of these commandments. Ask your father or mother to read them to you from Exodus 20. They command us to love God more than anyone else and to love our neighbor as much as we love ourselves.

God is our refuge and strength, a very present help in trouble.

— PSALM 46:1

IN BIBLE TIMES God commanded that there be cities of refuge. There were six of these cities. A city of refuge was a place of safety where someone could run if they had killed another person by accident. You can imagine that if a man killed someone, even by accident, there might be some relatives of the dead person coming after him to harm or maybe even kill him. But this man could quickly run to a city of refuge, and he would be safe. No one would be allowed to harm him there. But if he stepped outside of the city of refuge, his enemies would be allowed to hurt him. It was not safe for him to leave the city.

Children, we also must flee to a city of refuge, for we are all sinners. We have sinned against God's law. The law of God says that therefore we must die. Our only hope is to flee by faith to Jesus Christ, who is God's city of refuge for guilty sinners.

We have three great enemies which seek to have us — sin, Satan, and our own evil hearts. There are many sinful things in the world today for our eyes to see and our ears to hear, and also many sinful things to do. Satan is always trying to tempt us to sin. He tries to make sin not look so bad, and our evil hearts are willing to do evil rather than good.

But there is something wonderful. Although our enemies are mighty, God is almighty. In Jesus Christ, God is a perfect refuge. He is the only safe place for us to hide to escape these powerful enemies. We must stay near to God. In James 4:8 we read, "Draw nigh to God, and he will draw nigh to you." How do we stay near to God? By praying to Him, repenting before Him, believing in Him, and worshiping Him. God is able to give these gifts to us. The closer we stay to God, the safer we are; but if we wander away from Him, then we will be in danger just as the killer was in danger if he left the city of refuge.

Happy is he that hath the God
of Jacob for his help.

— PSALM 146:5a

Jacob was a man who lived in Bible times. He did not worship idols, which are pretend gods made out of wood or stone. He worshiped the living God.

Jacob had a new heart. He loved God and hated sin. He belonged to God and God belonged to him.

The Bible says that people who have the God of Jacob are happy. Does this mean that they always feel happy, that they have an easy life, that everything goes the way they want, and that they never have problems or pain? No, what it means is that they are happy because they have Jesus Christ as their Savior, their sins are forgiven, and when they do have troubles they have a place to go. They can kneel and fold their hands and tell God all their problems and ask Him to help them. God has promised to help those who call upon Him in truth with a sincere heart.

Jacob prayed and wrestled with God and God helped and blessed him. He can help and bless you too, and make you truly happy as you pray to Him.

Most things in this world cost money, but God does not make you give Him money before He answers your prayers. God wants your heart, your whole heart. God wants you to love Him more than everything and everyone else. Only when you glorify Him by giving Him your love and your heart, can you be truly happy. Can you do this by yourself? No. But God can move you to do so.

Pray that God will give you a new heart, a heart that loves Him more than all other things. Ask God to be your God and make you truly happy.

I am the way,
the truth,
and the life.

— JOHN 14:6a

WHAT DID JESUS mean when He said, "I am the way?" The way to whom, to what? He meant the way to God the Father, the way to eternal life.

Children, you remember that when God created Adam and Eve, He gave them a beautiful garden to live in, the Garden of Eden. He told them they could eat the fruit of all the trees except for one tree. That was the tree of the knowledge of good and evil. God told them if they disobeyed and ate the fruit of this tree, they would surely die.

Adam and Eve were perfectly happy living with God and with all He had given them. One day, however, Satan, the great enemy of God, came to Eve in the form of a serpent and told her a lie about eating the fruit of the tree of knowledge of good and evil. He said to her, "Ye shall not surely die, for God doth know that in the day ye eat thereof, then your eyes shall be opened, and ye shall be as gods, knowing good and evil" (Genesis 3:4–5). Adam and Eve believed Satan's lie rather than God's word. God's word is truth. By disobeying God and eating the fruit of the tree they were told not to eat, Adam and Eve separated themselves from God and were now afraid of Him. They remembered His command, so they ran away to hide from Him, expecting to die. Adam and Eve died spiritually. There would also now come a day that Adam and Eve would have to die physically. Then their bodies would die and be buried in the ground.

Then something amazing happened. God called Adam. Why did He call him? He must kill Adam and Eve, must He not? Adam was trembling behind the trees. But what does God do? Finding them, does He raise a knife to kill them? No, instead God kills an animal, pouring out its blood (its life) until it died, showing that by the shedding of the blood of another there is forgiveness of sins. And with the skin of this animal God made clothes for Adam and Eve to cover their nakedness, which they had tried to cover with the leaves of trees. The blood of the animal did not wash away their sin, but God showed them that without the shedding of blood there is no forgiveness of sins. He told Adam and Eve to look forward to the Savior who would one day be born on earth to live a sinless life and to suffer and die on the cross to pay for the sins of His people. His name is Jesus, which means Savior, "for he shall save his people from their sins" (Matthew 1:20).

So Jesus is the *way* back to God. He is the *truth* whose word never fails and who is always right and sure, not like Satan who always lies. And He is the *life,* for true Christians not only learn to find life in Jesus, but also learn to live out of Him by faith. Pray that Jesus Christ may be your Savior too! When you pray to God, always say at the end of your prayer, "For Jesus' sake, Amen."

Jesus answered and said unto him, Verily, verily, I say unto thee, Except a man be born again, he cannot see the kingdom of God.

— JOHN 3:3

WHAT DOES JESUS mean when He tells us that we must be born again? Must we enter our mother's womb again and be born a second time? No, Jesus means that we must be born again to God.

When we are born into this world, then we live for the things of this world. We live selfishly. We care most about ourselves and our pleasure. Our hearts go after all that we see, all of the toys of this world, and we do not love God. But when we are born again, the Holy Spirit comes to live in our heart, and a new life begins within us. We begin to live our life in a new way. We no longer live for the toys and things of the world. Our deepest desire is no longer to please ourselves. Now we love God and the things of another world, the upper world, heaven, and all that is in it. Now God becomes our best friend, and we need and want Him.

Newborn babies cry for their mother's milk. They are hungry and want to be fed. Spiritual life is like that. When a person is born again, he also cries. He cries for God, whom he now loves, and he longs to have God near him, just as a baby longs to be near its mother. He is made hungry and thirsty to know about God and His Son, Jesus Christ. In Psalm 42:2, David says, "My soul thirsteth for God."

Now where can a born-again person find God? He must have God! Children, he finds God in His Word, the Bible. The Bible is like milk to a born-again person, and when he reads it and the Holy Spirit brings the Word into his heart, showing him the precious Savior, then it is like drink for his thirsty soul. He is happy when he finds Christ as his Savior in the Bible, for God has fed his hungry soul with Himself.

Children, ask if you too may be born again, be made thirsty for the living God, and be satisfied only with Jesus Christ. Then you too will see and become a citizen of God's kingdom.

Keep thy tongue from evil.

— PSALM 34:13a

OUR TONGUE is a very small part of our body. It is a gift from God, and with it we are to praise and bless God. We can also help others with it. Each day at school your teacher speaks to you and teaches you through the use of her tongue. Each Sunday the minister's tongue is used by God to teach us the way of salvation. Your mother and father use their tongues each day to tell you they love you, to teach you who God is, who we are, and how we may be saved in Jesus Christ. God has given us a tongue so that we may pray to Him, "God be merciful to me a sinner" (Luke 18:13).

Now all these are good ways to use our tongue,

but there is also an evil way which we use far too often. The Bible tells us that our tongue is like a deadly poison. We often sin with it. When we tease a classmate or whisper something unkind about our teacher to a friend, we are speaking evil. We also sin at home when we fight with our brothers and sisters and call each other names. This is not keeping our tongue from evil. Have there also been times when we have lied to our father and mother? Perhaps your mother has asked you if you were the one who took the candy out of the cupboard, and you may have quickly said "No," which you knew was a lie. Does it bother you that sin slips easily off of our tongue, even though God commands us to keep our tongue from evil?

Many people use God's name wrongly when they become angry. They use God's name without reverence or respect, and even curse. This is terrible. Children, never do this. God is a holy God. We must only use God's name in prayer or when we are speaking with reverence and respect about our Creator.

A large ship is turned by the wheel or helm in the captain's hand. If he turns the helm the wrong

way, the ship can be in danger. Right turns of the wheel, however, can steer the ship safely into the harbor. Our tongue is like that wheel. If we use our tongue to speak evil, it can lead us or others into great danger, but when we use our tongue to speak well, it can do others and ourselves good.

The best use we can make of our tongue is to pray. Ask the Lord each day to help you speak good and not evil.

Look unto me, and be ye saved.

— ISAIAH 45:22a

IF YOU WERE DYING from a deadly disease, you would quickly go to the doctor for help. You would listen very carefully to what he told you to do, and then you would faithfully do all that he said. You would do anything if it would only help you to fight the disease.

But now, children, did you realize that you, by nature, are dying from a deadly disease? Each and every one of us is. This disease is called sin, and it has been passed on to us by our parents, Adam and Eve. When they ate the forbidden fruit, they sinned against God. God had said to Adam, "Thou shalt not eat of it; for in the day that thou eatest thereof thou shalt surely die" (Genesis 2:17b). Their souls turned from God to sin, their bodies would now die and return to the dust from which God made them, and their souls would perish forever in hell if they did not repent and did not believe in God's way of salvation.

We are no different from Adam and Eve. We eat the forbidden fruit every day, every time we choose to do evil rather than good. We, too, are sinning. This also means that our body will die. Our poor soul will also die forever in hell if we

continue in sin and do not repent. We need to have faith in Jesus Christ.

But our text is a beautiful one with hope. "Look unto me, and be ye saved, all the ends of the earth: for I am God, and there is none else." "Look" means to trust, or to believe in God alone. Just as the Israelites who were bitten by snakes in the wilderness were healed when they looked to a brazen serpent that Moses set up on a pole, so poor sinners like us who look to, or trust in, Jesus on Calvary's cross, shall be healed and saved from the deadly disease of sin. If we, by grace, look to Jesus Christ, God will forgive our sins, through His dear Son Jesus Christ, so we can live forever in heaven with God.

We need the Holy Spirit to make us understand that we are dying from the deadly disease of sin. We must ask for true repentance (sorrow about our sins), and then we will cry out, "Oh God, I look to Thee; Jesus, save me, there is no God like Thee to help and save me."

Make a joyful noise unto God, all ye lands.

— PSALM 66:1

DEAR CHILDREN, have you ever been awakened by the singing of the birds? These little creatures that the Lord God has made wake early in the morning, and the first thing they do is sing. It seems there is not one that does not sing, nor do they sing half-heartedly, but they all sing loudly, making a joyful noise to the Lord, singing the praises of their Creator.

What an example the birds are for us! We also should make a joyful noise to the Lord in the morning when we get out of our beds. Each of us must stop and ask ourselves, "Do I do this when I wake in the morning? Are my first thoughts of

God, thanking Him for His Son and gospel, and that I may wake to a new day?"

Have you ever taken time to think about how good the Lord is to you? Haven't you heard the gospel of salvation in Jesus already hundreds of times in your young life? Millions of boys and girls have never heard even once the good news about Jesus saving sinners. Don't you have a Bible to read and a church to go to where you may hear the Bible explained? Thousands of boys and girls have no Bible, no church, and no minister to explain the Word of God to them.

Are you lying sick in a bed or dying as many children are in hospitals? Do you have food to eat every day? Many children die every day because they have no food to eat. Do you have parents who love you, clothe you, and give you a home in which to live? There are many children who have been left with no parents, no home, and have only rags for clothes. Oh children, the Lord is so good to you. How worthy He is that we should make a joyful noise to Him each day!

"Praise God from whom all blessings flow, praise Him all creatures here below."

No man can serve two masters.

— MATTHEW 6:24a

THE LORD JESUS once told a story about a rich young ruler. One day this young man came to Jesus, asking what he could do to be sure that he might go to heaven. Jesus told him that he must keep the Ten Commandments. The rich young ruler said he had kept all of these commandments since he was a child. Children, do you know who was the only person here on earth who kept the Ten Commandments perfectly?

Jesus told the young man that he must sell all that he had and give the money to the poor people around him. Now the rich young man had a problem. He loved all the things that he owned.

No doubt he had many nice possessions because we read in the Bible that he was rich. Jesus was searching the young man's heart to see what the young man loved more, his worldly goods or Jesus who made heaven. We read in the Bible that the young man went away sad. He wanted the gift of heaven but not the giver of that gift, Jesus Christ.

Boys and girls, no one can serve two masters. We cannot give our hearts both to God and to the world. This rich young ruler served the world and loved the things of this world. They had the first place in his heart, so he couldn't give his heart to God. They were his idols, which he loved more than God his Maker. God wants the love of our hearts to go to Him and not to the things of the world. God says in His Word, "My son, give me thine heart" (Proverbs 23:26a).

How would you feel if your dear parents gave all their time and love to the things they owned and never gave you any attention or love? You would feel very sad. God is our Creator and Maker. He is the Father of all His creatures. He desires that we love and serve Him with our whole heart. Will you ask God for grace that you may love Him more than anyone or anything else?

Obey them that
have the rule
over you.

— HEBREWS 13:17a

WHAT WOULD YOU THINK of a farmer who did
not put a fence around his cow pasture? What
would happen to his cows? They would wander
away and would probably be killed on the road by
a car or truck. Or maybe some wild animals would
kill the cows and eat them. A farmer does not fence
in his cows to be cruel to them but to protect them.
Cows do not know how to keep themselves safe,
so the farmer must do it for them.

We also have a fence around us. It is not a fence
of wood or wire but a fence of words. These words
are the Ten Commandments. God gave us these
commandments to protect us from sin and harm.
God commands us to obey these words.

But children, many times throughout the day we break through this fence of God's law; often we do not obey but sin against God. The fifth commandment is "Honor thy father and thy mother" (Exodus 20:12a). This means we must obey them, for God has given them to rule and protect us. It is not always easy to obey our father and mother. Often we break this commandment. Think of the many things our mother and father ask us to do, or not to do:

"Do not fight with your brother or sister."

"Please pick up all of your toys."

"Do not talk to me that way."

How many times when you are told these things do you become angry and sometimes still disobey your parents? Or perhaps you obey with whining and complaining and a frown on your face, but not from your heart. Then you are breaking the fifth commandment and are not obeying them that have the rule over you, for your good.

Children, parents are a gift that the Lord has given you. They love you and want you to grow up to be not only good, obedient, hardworking children, but most important, children who are saved and who obey the Lord.

Once there was a boy whose parents let him do whatever he wanted to do. He could stay out as late as he wanted, but that boy was very sad. He longed for parents who loved him enough to give him rules to live by.

So now children, we must see that our parents' rules are given to us out of love, and God commands us to obey them from the heart. God has promised to bless those who do obey.

...Precious blood
of Christ.

— I PETER 1:19a

IF YOU WERE to fall on a sharp stone and get a cut on your leg that began to bleed a lot, would you continue to play? No, you would quickly go to your mother for help; and if she could not stop the bleeding, you would have to go to the doctor, and he would use medicine and bandages to make your leg better. God has given doctors and medicines to help us when our bodies are sick or injured.

Children, did you know that your soul has a deadly disease? It is called sin. It is deadly because if we do not receive medicine to heal this sore, then when we die we shall be separated from God and all His goodness to us forever. That is not good because then we will forever be with Satan, and Satan is not good and kind.

Our doctor here on earth cannot heal our deadly sore of sin, nor can his medicines. There is only one cure for this sore of sin, and that is the washing away of our sin in the precious blood of the Lord Jesus Christ. The blood of Jesus washes all sin away and makes our dirty hearts whiter than snow. How do we get this blood? Where do we go? Only Jesus can give it.

Now children, when you fall and cut your leg it begins to bleed. But what else happens? You begin to feel pain. And then you begin to cry, and you call for help. This is what happens when God shows His people their sore of sin. They feel pain in their soul because of their sin and they begin to cry. They call to God for help: "God be merciful to me a sinner" (Luke 18:13b), "Wash me and I shall be whiter than snow" (Psalm 51:7b), "Create in me a clean heart, O God" (Psalm 51:10b), "Heal my soul; for I have sinned against thee" (Psalm 41:4b). When God the Father hears a sinner's heartfelt cry, He pours Jesus' precious blood on his soul and creates a new, clean, spiritual heart.

Pray, children, that the Lord will show you your sore of sin and help you to flee to the precious blood of Jesus for salvation.

Quit you like men,
be strong.
— 1 CORINTHIANS 16:13b

IF WE WERE to make this verse easier for you to understand, we would write: "Behave like men, be strong." Now children, can we be strong without God? No, for God said in His Word, "Without me ye can do nothing" (John 15:5b). But He has also said, "With God all things are possible" (Matthew 19:26b). Remember the young boy David, who killed the giant Goliath with only a sling and a stone; or the three young men named Shadrach, Meshach, and Abednego, who refused to bow down to King Nebuchadnezzar's golden image, knowing that if they refused, they would be thrown into the burning fiery furnace? Did this bravery come from themselves? No, it came from God. When these young men were given new hearts, three gifts of grace were planted in their hearts—faith, love, and hope. They were given faith in God. Faith in God is to believe in Jesus Christ for salvation and to trust God with our lives. They believed that God would take care of them better than they could take care of themselves. They were given love for God. He became very precious to them, and they wanted to please Him. They were also given hope that their almighty God would protect and save them. They said to the king, "Our God whom we serve is able to deliver us from the burning fiery furnace, and he will deliver us out of thine hand, O king" (Daniel 3:17).

Now children, this story shows us the secret of the strength of God's children. Did Shadrach, Meshach, and Abednego put these words in their own hearts and mouths? No, almighty God gave them these words to say. He also gave them faith to believe their words to the king. They were given such love for God that they could not bow down to any other god. God put His strength in them. He made them brave, so that they could behave like men and be strong.

Each one of us needs these gifts of grace put into our hearts: faith in God, love for God, and hope in God. Pray to God that He may give you these gifts in Jesus Christ, so that you may grow up to be a strong, spiritual young man or woman. Never forget that Jesus paid the price for these gifts by dying on the cross so that God could give His children grace and strength to help in time of need.

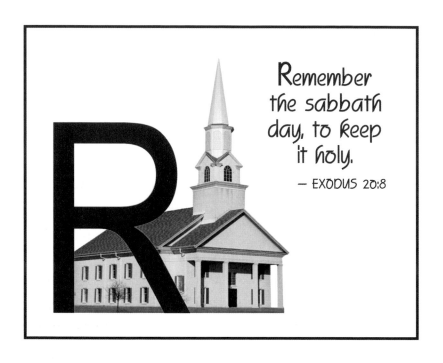

Remember the sabbath day, to keep it holy.

— EXODUS 20:8

DEAR CHILDREN, when we drive through the streets of our city as we go to church on the Lord's day, we see that almost every store is open, and people are going in and coming out. Not many years ago most of the stores were closed. Some had signs in the window saying "Store is closed—church is open." Many people were seen walking or driving to God's house. Today, instead of going to church on Sunday, we see many children playing ball, skating, or riding their bikes as on any other day. This ought not be, children. It disappoints God. The Lord gave the Sabbath day as a precious gift to us. What a wonderful gift

God has given us when He commanded us to set aside one day each week to do nothing but worship Him. As a nation, we have taken this gift and stepped on it. We have thrown it back at God and said, "We do not want this day as a day to seek and worship God. We will do with this day as we want to do." This makes God very sad.

The Bible tells us that God created the world in six days. He rested the seventh day and made it a holy day of rest, different from the other days of the week. On this day God promises to meet with us and bless us as we gather in His house. God gave us this day as a day of rest in which we must stop all unnecessary work and use the day to learn about Him, to honor Him, and to thank Him. We must go to God's house to hear what He will say to us in His Word and in the things that the minister says to remind us about the way God wants us to believe, think, and behave. The way of salvation in Jesus Christ is preached in God's house.

When church is over and we come home, we should talk with our parents about the sermon, the catechism class, or the Sunday School. We should also take time to seek God by studying the Bible, learning verses from it, or by reading instructive books written by God's people. It is also good to visit grandparents and people in nursing homes on Sunday, to speak about God and His Word.

If we want God to bless us on the Sabbath, we must be where God promises to be, asking Him to rain down His Holy Spirit upon us. Is that at the store, or off playing ball with friends, or while reading worldly books, where God's name is never mentioned? No, it is when we are seeking God where His name is heard or while praying to God, that God blesses us. Children, please remember always to keep the Sabbath holy.

Seek ye the Lord while he may be found.

— ISAIAH 55:6a

DEAR CHILDREN, did you know that this is the most important thing we must do in our lives? God tells us in His Word, "But seek ye first the kingdom of God, and his righteousness; and all these things shall be added unto you" (Matthew 6:33). If we seek God, and, by grace, find Him, He makes us His children. Then He will give us everything that we need for our soul and body.

How can we seek God? First, we must pray. That is how we may talk to God and ask Him for a new heart. We must ask God to show us how sinful we are and to give us faith to believe in Jesus.

We must also seek God in His Word, the Bible.

God gave us His Word to teach us about ourselves, how sinful and unclean our hearts are; but His Word also teaches us that God sent His Son to be a Savior for sinners, bringing them to repentance, making them deeply sorry for their sins, and giving them faith and desire to serve God with all their heart. We cannot see God, but as we read the Bible we learn who He is, and we learn about the wonderful works He does for His children. God speaks to His children through the Bible. The Holy Spirit brings that word into His child's soul, filling him with faith and hope in God, and love for his God and Father.

Another way we can seek God is to be in church when God's Word is being preached or taught, in sermons, in catechism class, or in Sunday

School. We should often be found in God's house because God is pleased to meet us there. We can also seek God at home during family or personal devotions and through Christian education. God says in His Word, "For where two or three are gathered together in my name, there am I in the midst of them" (Matthew 18:20). Isn't that a wonderful promise from God? He promises that whenever two or more people gather together to hear or speak about the Lord and His ways, God will be there to bless them.

"Seek ye the Lord," says our text, "while he may be found." The day is coming, children, when God may not be found. Some people try to seek the Lord when they are old, but cannot find Him. Now, when you are young, is the time to seek the Lord. The best time to seek God is always today. Tomorrow may be too late. None of us knows if we will be living tomorrow, nor do we know when Jesus Christ is coming on the clouds.

Ask the Lord to give you grace and wisdom to seek Him and to call on Him today, while you are young. He has promised, "Those that seek me early shall find me" (Proverbs 8:17b).

Teach me thy way,
O Lord, and lead me in a plain path.

— PSALM 27:11a

HAVE YOU EVER taken a walk through the woods on a path that you knew very well? You may have noticed many smaller paths leading off the path you followed. Sometimes you were tempted to take one of these smaller paths to see where it would lead you. But as it brought you deeper into the woods, you became frightened and quickly went back to the main, plain path that would bring you safely home.

This is a lesson for us, children. There is one main path that leads to God, and we must look for, and stay on, that path.

We do not choose this path, by nature, because

our sinful nature makes us selfish and greedy. We do not seek God's kingdom first, but we go down the smaller paths in life to build up our own kingdom. We try to find all of our joy and happiness in the things of this world. Our hearts desire one toy after another. One week we want this toy, the next week we want another toy. We are going from one path to another path. Soon we have our toys all around us, but we are far away from God. Can all of our toys give us a new heart? Can they bring us to faith in Jesus Christ and repentance before God? Can they teach us how to serve God and live thankfully before Him? Can they bring us into heaven to be with God forever when we die? No, children, only Jesus can do this for us. We need to ask Him to set our feet on the right path that will lead us to Him.

Unite my heart to fear thy name.

— PSALM 86:11b

HAVE YOU EVER noticed the things your mother does for you? She does them all because she loves you. She washes the clothes and teaches you to put them neatly away so that you will have clean clothes to put on each day. Every day she makes sure you have the good foods your body needs so that you have energy to do your work. She teaches you to keep your home neat and orderly so that you may live comfortably. She teaches you to wash and dry the dishes so that the next time you eat you will have a clean plate on which to put your food. Even when she goes shopping, she is doing this for your good so that you will have food to eat and clothes to wear. Mothers do all these things because they love their families.

Children, this is what our text is about. It says, "Unite my heart to fear thy name." Another way to say this is, "Bring me to love Thee with my whole heart. Let all that I do each day be done out of childlike fear to Thee and to serve Thee, O God."

If the Lord were to convert a little girl (that is, give her a new spiritual heart), her life would begin to change. She would begin to hate sin, to love and fear God. She would want to please God more than anyone else. She would get more joy from God's smiles of approval than from the smiles of people. She would be more afraid of God's frowns of disapproval than the frowns of people. People who fear God love to please God.

This girl would also be more helpful to her mother, because in helping her mother she would be serving God. She would be kind to her classmates even when she was treated unkindly because God says, "Be ye kind one to another" (Ephesians 4:32a). She would fear and serve God by obeying His word. If she were tempted to do something naughty, she would turn away because God says, "Depart from evil and do good" (Psalm 37:27a). She would serve God rather than Satan. Before she was converted, she did not listen very well in church or catechism. After her conversion she would listen very closely, hoping that God would teach her His ways and lead her in His path so she may learn to serve Him more and more. At bedtime she would read her Bible and pray to God before going to sleep, because she loves Him and wants to end her day seeking and talking with her God. God has joined her heart to His and brought her to love Him.

When this little girl sinned, she would be sad and ask God's forgiveness. She would be sad because she disobeyed God, and because her whole heart was not serving God. God's children hate sin, and long to serve God perfectly, with their whole heart.

What would you think of a mother who did everything for her family except feed them? You would think she must not love them with her whole heart. Children, it is not enough if we go to church and catechism and listen closely to our Bible story in school. God desires us to fear and serve Him with our whole heart in all that we do. Ask God to unite your heart to fear His name and bring you to do all things each day to serve Him with joy and love.

Verily there is a reward for the righteous.

— PSALM 58:11a

GOD'S CHILDREN have many enemies. In God's Word these enemies are called foes. There are many examples in the Bible of God's righteous children being treated unkindly by these foes. Righteous Noah was mocked for building an ark on dry land, at God's command. Righteous Daniel was cast into the den of lions because he prayed to God rather than to King Darius. Boys and girls, we must never mock anyone, but it is especially sinful to mock God's servants.

Our verse tells us that there is a reward for the righteous, yet it seems as though these men suffered for their righteousness and were not rewarded. If we read further, however, we see that God does reward His children. Noah lived because he obeyed God and completed the ark. He did not stop obeying God even when he was being mocked. What became of Daniel in the lions' den? God shut the mouths of the lions so that in the morning Daniel was brought out alive.

Most of all, however, Noah and Daniel were rewarded, by God's grace, with a sense of God's blessing in their souls. They had an inward sense of peace with God through the Messiah even when they were being mocked. God rewards obedience with inward peace.

So children, do you now see the reward of the righteous? By God's grace, it is not only life, but God's blessing and favor in Jesus Christ. His blessing and favor are more than life, David said. Yes, God's blessing and favor lead to the best reward of all—the gracious reward of enjoying the triune God forever in the place of eternal life that we call heaven.

All of these rewards are God's gracious gifts that He is pleased to give the righteous. No one—not even Noah or Daniel—earns such rewards, for even the righteous, at their very best, do no more than is their duty to do and also still sin in this life.

Wash me, and I shall be whiter than snow.

— PSALM 51:7b

DEAR CHILDREN, do you remember a wintry morning when you looked outside your window and you could not believe how beautiful everything looked with a blanket of fresh snow? Whiteness everywhere! Everything looked so pure and clean. But it did not stay beautiful for very long, did it? Soon after, the snow became brown when dirt and mud were mixed with it.

This is a picture of our spiritual hearts. God created Adam and Eve each with a clean heart, but when they chose to disobey God, they made their hearts dirty with sin. We are no different from Adam and Eve. We also choose to disobey

God each day, and our hearts become more and more filled with filthy sin.

In nature the snow melts away, showing the brown earth, but soon a new white blanket of snow again covers the earth, and once more everything looks clean and beautiful. In this way our wise Creator makes the earth clean again.

Children, our spiritual hearts need the same thing again and again. Our hearts are filled with all of the sins that we commit and have committed day after day. We need to see how hateful these sins are to a holy and righteous God, and that we are lost sinners before Him. When a lost sinner feels how dirty his heart is with sin, he cries out to God, "Wash me, and I shall be whiter than snow."

In God's time, Jesus, who is called the Sun of righteousness, comes and fills the sinner with the warmth of His love. Jesus shows the sinner that, because He died on the cross for lost sinners, their sins will be washed away in the cleansing blood of Jesus and their hardened hearts melted to love God. Then the forgiven sinner is covered with the robe of Jesus' righteousness, which is *whiter* than snow.

EXamine me,
O Lord,
and prove me.

— PSALM 26:2a

HAVE YOU EVER looked at yourself in the mirror when the light in the room is turned off? You cannot see very much of yourself, can you? Maybe you can just barely see the outline of your face and of your body. What a difference there is when you turn the light on! Then you can see everything clearly.

Children, when we do not love the Lord Jesus and are unconverted, it is very dark in our heart. It is like a room with the lights turned off. We cannot see our sin and how evil we are. But if God gives us a new heart, He sends His Holy Spirit to live in us. The Holy Spirit sheds light in our heart, and we begin to see our sin. We learn who God is—a holy and righteous God who hates sin. The Holy Spirit teaches us about God's law, the Ten Commandments, and we begin to see how bad we are, for we find ourselves always disobeying God's laws. The Ten Commandments are like a mirror in our heart, and when we look into that mirror and try to see how good we are, we only see how sinful we are.

If you had a big sore on your face, and you looked in the mirror when the light was off, it would not scare you much. But if you turned the light on and saw the bloody sore, what would you do? You would probably call to your mother for help, and together you would try to wash it and then find medicine to heal it and bandages to cover it.

It is like that when the Holy Spirit shines light on our sin. We cry out, "Oh, how awful sin is! Oh, what a mess my heart is!" We try to clean up our sin, we try not to sin, and then we try to cover up our sin with our bandages of good works. We try to see how many good things we can do to make up for all our sinfulness. But the Holy Spirit keeps shining more and more light on our hearts, showing more and more sin. He shows us that even the good things we do come from an evil heart.

Happily, the Holy Spirit also shows us that Jesus Christ is the Savior who by His death saves poor sinners from all their sins. Jesus' blood is a better healing medicine than our good works, for His blood is accepted by God the Father, to whom He was perfectly obedient in all His sufferings.

In our text, "Examine me, O Lord, and prove me," David is asking God to shine light on his heart again so that David can see if there is any sin in his heart that may make God sad. David loves God and wants to please God by obeying all of God's commandments.

That is true of everyone who has learned to love God and the Lord Jesus as his Savior. All God's people want God to examine them, to correct them from every evil way, and to lead them in God's paths of holiness.

Children, ask God to work in your heart so that you will long to be examined by God and walk in His ways.

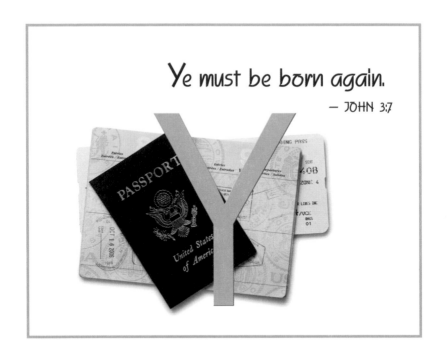

Ye must be born again.

— JOHN 3:7

HAVE YOU EVER heard of places called China, Russia, Germany, or the Netherlands? These far-away places are called foreign countries. People usually travel to them by flying in a big airplane. Someday you will probably travel to a foreign country, but before you go you will have to get a passport. A passport is a little book which has your picture in it, along with some information about you. Without a passport you would not be allowed into a foreign country. When you would come up to the gate and ask to go into the country, someone would ask, "May I please see your passport?" And if you said, "I do not have one," you would be told that you may not go in. What a disappointment that would be, to travel all that way, hoping to go in, and then to be sent away.

Children, we read in God's Word of another country that is not a part of this world. This country is heaven, God's kingdom. God sits on His throne in heaven, and all His children who have died on earth are now around Him there, worshiping and singing, "Holy, holy, holy, LORD God Almighty" (Revelation 4:8). They adore their King who has saved them from all of their enemies, and now they may live with Him forever.

We read in God's Word of what a beautiful place heaven is. The walls and streets are made of gold and precious jewels. There is no sorrow or sin in heaven, only joy and love, because God is there.

Now children, you may wonder, "How may I come to this beautiful country to be with God forever when I die?" To enter heaven you must have a passport. But this is a different passport. This passport is the blood of Jesus. To have this passport, we need to be born again, and need to have all our faith for salvation placed only in Jesus and His redeeming blood.

God says, "Ye must be born again." God means that when we were first born, we were born with a sinful heart. Satan was the god whom we loved and obeyed. But when a sinner is born again, God enters the sinner's heart, and Satan is no longer his king. He now has a new heart and everything changes for that sinner. He begins to hate sin and, at the same time, is given a love for God and His Word. God becomes the one whom he loves and worships. He believes in Jesus Christ alone for salvation and finds his all in this precious Savior. Like Peter, he learns to speak of Christ's blood as "precious blood" (1 Peter 1:19), and comes to understand that only by that blood—that is, by Jesus dying in his place—can he receive heaven's passport. Everything becomes new in Jesus Christ; it is as if that sinner is beginning life all over again. That is why it is called being born again.

To come into that heavenly country where God is king, we must first have Jesus be in our heart here on earth. Pray that God would give you the new life in Christ.

Zion heard, and was glad.

— PSALM 97:8a

DEAR CHILDREN, God has many children here on earth. God's children are people whom He has chosen to save in Jesus Christ, and to give His Holy Spirit to teach them to live a holy life. God loves each one of His children, and He takes care of them. He supplies them with all of their needs.

God's people are scattered throughout the whole world. Wherever God's Word is brought, God is pleased to visit the souls of people and cause some of them to truly love Him. Missionaries go to far-away places to preach to the men, women, and children in cities and jungles.

Children, if we live in the United States or Canada, we are called Americans or Canadians; the people in China are called Chinese. Did you know there is also another name for God's children? They are called Zion, and the Lord God is their King. He is the King of Zion. The King of Zion has two places where He rules. One place is in heaven, the country of Zion, where all His people who have died are now praising Him; but He also is pleased to dwell in His Zion here on earth in His church in the hearts of His people. When God speaks His Word to them, they are filled with joy. Therefore our verse says, "Zion heard, and was glad."

Children, our prayer for each of you is that God may make you one of the people of Zion. Then when you die, you also may enter the country of Zion, heaven, to worship the holy and blessed tri-une God forever. Then you will be eternally glad in and with Jesus Christ, and enjoy communion with all of the people of Zion and the holy angels.

Conclusion

WE HOPE BY NOW you see how much your soul is worth and how important it is to take care of it. We also hope you see how the Bible verses in this book are helpful for knowing how to take care of your soul. Let us encourage you to continue to re-member Bible verses. Remember what they mean and trust God to use them to save your soul from sin's evil works.

The Bible verses in this book are not the only verses that are important for spiritual life. They are a good place to start, but all of God's Word is important. You should not stop hiding God's Word in your heart with the verses in this book. You should also read and memorize other verses from the Bible. Make it your goal to understand and treasure the Bible as a way to give your soul life and keep your heart safe.

My son, attend to my words; incline thine ear unto my sayings. Let them not depart from thine eyes; keep them in the midst of thine heart. For they are life unto those that find them, and health to all their flesh. Keep thy heart with all diligence; for out of it are the issues of life.

—Proverbs 4:20–23

APPENDIX
More Words for Life

Here are more Bible verses for you to work on. Try to memorize, understand, and treasure them. These verses remind us of the greatness of God, the problem of our sins, salvation in Jesus, and the faithful life of a Christian.

- The heavens declare the glory of God; and the firmament sheweth his handywork.

  — PSALM 19:1

- LORD, our Lord, how excellent is thy name in all the earth! who hast set thy glory above the heavens.

  — PSALM 8:1

- In the beginning God created the heaven and the earth.

  — GENESIS 1:1

- So God created man in his own image, in the image of God created he him; male and female created he them.

  — GENESIS 1:27

71

- My son, forget not my law; but let thine heart keep my commandments. — PROVERBS 3:1

- But your iniquities have separated between you and your God, and your sins have hid his face from you, that he will not hear. — ISAIAH 59:2

- As it is written, There is none righteous, no, not one: There is none that understandeth, there is none that seeketh after God. — ROMANS 3:10–11

- For the wrath of God is revealed from heaven against all ungodliness and unrighteousness of men, who hold the truth in unrighteousness. —ROMANS 1:18

- For the wages of sin is death; but the gift of God is eternal life through Jesus Christ our Lord. — ROMANS 6:23

- For God so loved the world, that he gave his only begotten Son, that whosoever believeth in him should not perish, but have everlasting life. — JOHN 3:16

- For when we were yet without strength, in due time Christ died for the ungodly. — ROMANS 5:6

- All we like sheep have gone astray; we have turned every one to his own way; and the LORD hath laid on him the iniquity of us all.

  — ISAIAH 53:6

- For there is one God, and one mediator between God and men, the man Christ Jesus; who gave himself a ransom for all, to be testified in due time.

  —1 TIMOTHY 2:5–6

- For whosoever shall call upon the name of the Lord shall be saved.

  — ROMANS 10:13

- Then spake Jesus again unto them, saying, I am the light of the world: he that followeth me shall not walk in darkness, but shall have the light of life.

  — JOHN 8:12

- Thy word is a lamp unto my feet, and a light unto my path.

  —PSALM 119:105

- And thou shalt love the LORD thy God with all thine heart, and with all thy soul, and with all thy might.

  — DEUTERONOMY 6:5

- And as ye would that men should do to you, do ye also to them likewise.

  — LUKE 6:31

- Rejoice evermore. Pray without ceasing. In every thing give thanks: for this is the will of God in Christ Jesus concerning you.

  — 1 THESSALONIANS 5:16–18

- Finally, brethren, whatsoever things are true, whatsoever things are honest, whatsoever things are just, whatsoever things are pure, whatsoever things are lovely, whatsoever things are of good report; if there be any virtue, and if there be any praise, think on these things.

  — PHILIPPIANS 4:8

- Give thanks unto the LORD; for he is good: because his mercy endureth for ever.

  — PSALM 118:1